The Riverside Church
IN THE
City of
New York

Table of Contents

"Prophetic, germinative ideas are here; there are open doors of possibility for good as well as evil..."

Harry Emerson Fosdick

Foreword

"Nothing that is worth doing can be achieved in our lifetime; therefore we must be saved by hope. Nothing which is true or beautiful or good makes complete sense in any immediate context of history; therefore we must be saved by faith. Nothing we do, however virtuous, can be accomplished alone; therefore we are saved by love."

Reinhold Niebuhr

The Riverside Church of New York stands in gothic grandeur on the Upper West Side of Manhattan overlooking the Hudson River. At night its lighted tower can be seen from almost every direction in the city.

Since its dedication in 1931, worshippers from across the nation and around the world have streamed through the church's vaulted portals to find guidance, encouragement, and a call to peace, compassion, and hope.

One of Riverside's continuing challenges has been to make its message and ministries as inspiring and relevant as its edifice is beautiful. Ministers and prophetic voices from around the world are expected to challenge worshippers, ecclesiastical and corporate structures, and political leaders to "do justly, love mercy, and to walk humbly with God."

As an open and affirming congregation aligned with both the American Baptist Churches USA and the United Church of Christ, we stand in the rich tradition of prophetic Christianity. Over the years the community has come to expect cutting-edge commitment to the radical demands of the Gospel of Jesus Christ and forthrightness in speaking truth to power. We seek to be a congregation where the kingdom of God for which we pray is served by the constancy of our vibrant witness. We pray for the power of the Holy Spirit to help us keep faith with the hope expressed in the dedicating hymn (pg. 45) of our founder, Harry Emerson Fosdick:

> God of grace and God of glory,
> On Thy people pour Thy power;
> Crown Thine ancient church's story;
> Bring its bud to glorious flower.

Dr. James A. Forbes, Jr.

A Perspective

Six thousand people gathered at the west portal for the first Sunday service at The Riverside Church, October 5, 1930.

This day marked the culmination of one dream and the opening of doors to new ones.

The planning and construction of the new building was the work of six years, but the development of the church itself covered almost a century.

The church's story began as early as 1841 in a modest meeting house on the lower east side.

For decades the lay members and pastors sought to be a progressive church and to enrich the spiritual life of the wider community. More and more, people came to the doors.

Finding more than once that a larger building was needed for the expression of its ministry, this vigorous church moved farther and farther north like the rapidly expanding city itself.

From its earliest days the church was distinguished by its open-minded and outspoken ministers: George Benedict, pastor of the Norfolk Street Baptist Church from 1841 to 1848; Thomas B. Armitage, pastor from 1848 to 1889 of the new Fifth Avenue Baptist Church; W.H.P. Faunce, from 1889 to 1899; Rufus Johnston, from 1901 to 1906;

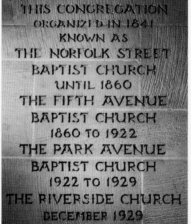

THIS CONGREGATION
ORGANIZED IN 1841
KNOWN AS
THE NORFOLK STREET
BAPTIST CHURCH
UNTIL 1860
THE FIFTH AVENUE
BAPTIST CHURCH
1860 TO 1922
THE PARK AVENUE
BAPTIST CHURCH
1922 TO 1929
THE RIVERSIDE CHURCH
DECEMBER 1929

Charles Aked, from 1907 to 1911; and Cornelius Woelfkin, from 1912 to 1926.

Under the wise and progressive leadership of Dr. Woelfkin, the Park Avenue Baptist Church provided the community a daily, year-round ministry. Over the years, members of the congregation had been struggling with the rising controversy between fundamentalism and modernism in the interpretation of the Bible. As Dr. Woelfkin prepared for retirement, they became deeply interested in the inspired preaching of Harry Emerson Fosdick. Dr. Fosdick had become a key figure in this debate, as a result of his sermon of May 21, 1922, at the First Presbyterian Church in New York City, titled "Shall the Fundamentalists Win?"

Led by John D. Rockefeller, Jr., an active layman in the church, the membership called Dr. Fosdick in 1925. He agreed, on three conditions.

First, affirmation of faith in Christ must be the only requirement for membership.

Second, any Christian, regardless of denomination, seeking admission to the church, must be freely welcomed.

Third, a new and larger building and a more expansive ministry should be planned in a neighborhood critical to the life of the whole city.

Harry Emerson Fosdick

The Park Avenue Baptist Church weighed seriously the terms of his acceptance, but proved itself ready for his challenge.

Dr. Fosdick and the congregation recognized a compelling need for a Protestant parish church to minister to the thousands of people drawn to Morningside Heights by Columbia University, Barnard College, Teachers College, Union Theological Seminary, the Jewish Theological Seminary, International House, and St. Luke's Hospital. A site was chosen and plans for the new building were drawn in 1926.

The building was financed primarily through the sale of properties of the church on Park Avenue and the generous donations of a few individuals, particularly John D. Rockefeller Jr., under whose leadership a building committee was established. Another valuable member of the committee was Eugene Carder, associate minister, who took great interest in every detail. Dr. Carder inspired the cooperation and enthusiasm of the committee, the architects and artists, the construction firm and its workers, and the people of the church. Each person with the slightest role in the undertaking was made to feel part of a noble endeavor.

The architects, Charles Collens and Henry C. Pelton, traveled through France and Spain to visit cathedrals and to assimilate the best architectural concepts of Gothic grandeur and contemporary usefulness.

The Riverside Church cornerstone was laid on November 20, 1927 and within a year the enormous nave was standing.

Laying of the cornerstone, November 20, 1927

7

There were difficulties ahead, particularly the devastating fire in the new nave, just prior to the closing sale of the Park Avenue site. But the congregation was well accustomed to challenge and would continue to grow from its firm foundation.

December 21, 1928, an electrical fire on the wooden scaffolding spread through the entire nave. This devastating experience caused a major delay on the building and a strain on the enthusiasm of the congregation.

There was one welcome result. Since the fire occurred just prior to the purchase of the still-occupied Park Avenue site by the Central Presbyterian Church, the congregation was left homeless as of July 1 of the following year. It was with surprised delight that they accepted the invitation of their Jewish friends at Temple Emanu-El to occupy the former synagogue of part of their congregation. Thus began a new adventure in the ecumenical spirit.

The true challenge in the building of The Riverside Church was that the magnificent facility be not only equaled but surpassed by the quality of the ministries that would grow out of it.

While still at the Park Avenue Church, Dr. Fosdick reminded the congregation: "Very frequently these days people come to me and say the new church will be wonderful. My friends, it is not settled yet whether or not the new church will be wonderful. That depends on what we do with it...."

Dr. Fosdick and the congregation set out to create a nonsectarian, inclusive church. The church maintained its affiliation with the American Baptist Churches USA and later would affiliate with the United Church of Christ. The congregation resolved to channel its gifts not through particular denominations alone but to individually selected causes in the community, the nation, and the world.

The church opened its doors to people of all races and nations, and sought to appeal to the needs and concerns of people of all economic backgrounds.

For its convictions to be solidly founded, the congregation determined to welcome diversity rather than tolerate it, to demonstrate a belief that liberty of the individual is based not on the idea that what one *is* is unimportant, but that it is too important to be regimented and controlled by external authority.

The Riverside Church made a commitment both to worship and to Christian service. A seven-day-a-week program sought to meet the spiritual, psychological, physical, and social needs of the community at large.

It was soon evident that the congregation need not attempt to impose a prearranged program on the community, for the community itself immediately recognized and responded to needs and initiated one program after another under the church's roof.

The first decade was one of experimentation. The depression of the 1930s was met with a remarkable relief program which contributed directly to the encouragement and employment of thousands.

A sewing workshop within the church employed women at $3.00 a day and prepared them for employment outside the church. This and other relief programs were the start of the Social Services Ministry.

The nursery school and expanded adult education and cultural programs were also started in response to the burden of the depression.

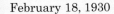

The sewing workshop (above) trained women at a skilled trade and prepared them for the work force at a critical time of widespread unemployment.

Also in response to the crippling needs of the depression, The Riverside Church established a relief program in cooperation with the State Labor Bureau and the Charity Organization Society. The program of placement and counseling involved the congregation directly in providing jobs, gave countless people a new start, and put thousands back to work.

The church outgrew all expectations, and all the predictions from the community, as to the number of children who would attend. The program flourished as hundreds of boys and girls spent Friday evenings and three hours on Sunday at the church, while related programs were developed for family counseling and adult education. Meanwhile, the church recognized a need, and began a weekday nursery school.

February 18, 1930

9

Organizations established before the move to Morningside Heights, such as the Women's Society, the Men's Class, and the Board of Ushers, preserved tradition and continued to grow in the new church. New programs also emerged. The Riverside Guild, the Business and Professional Women's Club, the Riverside Symphony Orchestra, and the Arts and Crafts program attested to the congregation's continual response to changing needs and interests.

Worship reflected the same freedom of expression in its variety of forms and religious traditions. A united purpose was clearly stated in the celebration of communion:

> There are in this church many members of many denominations and many faiths. In welcoming you into our membership, we do not ask you to give up any belief or form that is dear to you but rather to bring it to us that we may be enriched thereby. We invite you not to our table or the table of any denomination, but to the Lord's table.

To the thousands of people soon actively involved in The Riverside Church, Dr. Fosdick expressed the need for a church to be responsive to individuals. In his counseling and the preaching that grew largely out of it, Dr. Fosdick demonstrated a deep commitment to the individual which has remained central to the ministry of the church.

The Second World War brought new challenges. Now a firm pacifist, Dr. Fosdick not only preached against the evils of war, but also strived to help individuals keep their faith, integrity, and vision for a better world.

Dr. Fosdick's ministry during World War II was not limited to protest against war. The congregation corresponded with some 200 members in active service and were active in a variety of wartime services.

For 3-1/2 years the Naval Reserve Midshipmen's School, headquartered at Columbia University, used the facilities of The Riverside Church for recreation, athletics, and worship, with 2,000 attending each Sunday evening.

In 1945, when the war at last was over, the Riverside Fund to Build a Christian World was established to further the rehabilitation effort abroad.

Led by Dr. Fosdick, Father George Ford of Corpus Christi Roman Catholic Church, and Rabbi Lewis Finkelstein of the Jewish Theological Seminary, the congregation also joined with neighborhood groups to improve the blighted areas of their own community.

In 1947, Morningside Heights, Inc., a nonprofit membership corporation uniting fourteen institutions, including The Riverside Church, was founded to work for social and physical improvement of the area. The church offered its support to the newly-established Manhattanville Neighborhood Center.

Robert James McCracken, a Scottish minister teaching at McMaster University in Canada, was chosen to succeed Dr. Fosdick on his retirement in 1946. He, too, was soon widely known as a powerful preacher, a vigorous critic of military escalation, and an advocate of racial justice. He led the church in establishing a relationship with neighboring academic institutions and their students, and in responding to the needs of the city. During the ministry of Dr. McCracken, the church achieved significant growth in the participation of the laity in the governance and work of the church.

In 1953 a series of task forces, formed by the Board of Trustees and the Board of Deacons, reviewed the church's program. Their report strongly recommended an increased awareness of the distinct role a church could play in the lives of its members, the city, and the world.

When this report was published, it was evident that the opportunity for fulfillment of the church's original plan for expansion was now at hand.

10

The dedication of the South Wing in 1959 opened the doors of the church to a still wider community and to the challenge of the need for greater understanding of the cultural, political, and social goals of the many groups in the city.

Robert James McCracken

Civil rights leader Rev. Dr. Martin Luther King, Jr., (January 15, 1929 - April 4, 1968) preached at Riverside five times during the civil rights era. During one of those visits on August 13, 1961, King delivered the "Pauline Letter" urging all Christians to join the civil rights movement. In addition to those five times, he delivered his now famous *Beyond Vietnam* speech, during a conference of *Clergy and Layman Concerned about the War in Vietnam*, exactly one year before his assassination.

During the height of the civil rights movement, Riverside offered consistent support to Dr. King and provided an open pulpit for him to challenge the nation and its leaders. Riverside was very active in both the civil rights and anti-war movement and the Benevolence Committee made several grants to the Southern Christian Leadership Conference, while Dr. King was president.

> "...But at its best, the Church has spurned conformity with the world...It has not trimmed its message to current thought or to current social trends...it [has] created new ideals, new convictions, new characters, new power that made men different and made their generation different...The great epochs in the Church's history were not epochs when it made common cause with the world but when it stood over and against the world, fearlessly proclaiming the Word of God manifested in Jesus Christ."
>
> Robert J. McCracken

A year later, the church seized a special opportunity for a greater outreach as it obtained the license for the area's last available FM radio frequency. WRVR aimed to further cultural and political education, and initiated the weekly broadcasting of the Sunday morning service of worship and related programming.

Ernest T. Campbell came to the pulpit in 1968, following the retirement of Dr. McCracken. Born and reared in the neighborhood and familiar with its problems and opportunities, he brought to the church a distinctive emphasis on its role in the life of the city. During his ministry the contribution of the black membership of the church increased in vigor and significance, as did the stress on the church's need to confront the problems of racism and the Vietnam War. He continued his predecessors' tradition of excellence in preaching and their emphasis on the balance between social action and spiritual regeneration within a distinctively biblical framework.

The civil rights struggle of the nineteen sixties had a major bearing on the church and its self-understanding. With the addition to the staff of a minister of urban affairs, the church

11

William Sloane Coffin, Jr.

attempted to widen its outreach. Tension and misunderstanding mounted following the confrontation of the congregation at a nave service by black political activist James Forman in May 1969. In an effort toward an effective ministry to all races, the congregation established the Riverside Fund for Social Justice. In 1972 the congregation and the community raised $350,000 for a three-year project aimed to empower the powerless in urban society and to change the root causes of social injustice. In addition, programs committed to social justice, such as the Black Christian Caucus and the Prison Task Force, were started.

The eighteen-month Metropolitan Mission Study, concluded in 1974, again examined the church's ministry in a changing society. The study set forth four major emphases for members of the church: the use and distribution of power, corporate and individual; the elimination of racism; an understanding of the meaning and quality of human life; and the development of a Christian life-style.

In 1975 the church raised over $115,000 for the Riverside Intercultural Support for Education, aimed mainly at the support of black church-related colleges.

In 1976, on the resignation of Dr. Campbell, Jitsuo Morikawa was invited to assume leadership of the church in a one-year interim position as the church sought a new senior minister. Dr. Morikawa provided a nurturing spirit to a congregation in transition.

In the fall of 1977, The Riverside Church called William Sloane Coffin, Jr. to be Senior Minister.

Under the ministry of Dr. Coffin, who served until 1989, The Riverside Church again experienced the urgent summons of a new era, yet one that ironically recalled some of the concerns of the earlier troubled age of its first minister. At a time of widespread economic plight, the church sought to find ways to minister to the poor and

April 16, 1978, Rabbi Ronald Sobel of Temple Emanu-El preached from the Riverside pulpit. His sermon deplored the fact that at a great price institutions have not come fully to grips with prejudice.

Ernest T. Campbell broadcasting on National Radio Pulpit, continuing a tradition started by Dr. Fosdick on NBC radio's National Vespers.

"Moses, Moses."
"Mary, Mary."
"Riverside, Riverside."
The air is full of calls coming to us
At all times, in unexpected places...
And how many times, after some
resistance, will we find the grace to
answer, "Here am I," "Here we are"?

William Sloane Coffin, Jr.

Reconciliation Sunday, 1978, Riverside commemorated the sending of a shipload of wheat to Vietnam by churches and synagogues. The wheat, donated by midwest farmers, was symbolized in the communion service by a loaf of bread baked by Kansas Mennonites.

The Building

STAINED GLASS	MODELERS AND CARVERS
Reynolds, Francis & Rohnstock, Boston	Robert Garrison, Sculptor
Wilbur Herbert Burnham, Boston	Piccirilli Brothers, New York
Harry Wright Goodhue, Boston	John Donnelly & Co., New York
Charles Lorin, Chartres, France	Maxfield H. Keck, New York
Jacques Simon, Rheims, France	Charles H. Humphriss, New York
The D'Ascenzo Studios, Philadelphia	Alexander Ruel, New York
	George Brown & Company, Newark, N.J.

WOOD CARVING	ORGAN BUILDERS
William F. Ross & Co., East Cambridge, Mass.	Hook & Hastings, Kendall Green, Mass.
Irving & Casson, A.H. Davenport Co., New York	Aeolian-Skinner Organ Company
	Anthony A. Bufano
	Gilbert F. Adams

HANDWROUGHT IRON	CARILLON BELL FOUNDERS
Oscar B. Bach, New York	Gillett & Johnston, Croydon, England
Renner & Maras, New York	Van Bergen Foundry, Heiligerlee, Holland
	White Chapel Foundry, London, England

The South Wing

STAINED GLASS	MOSIACS
Charles J. Connick Associates	Charles J. Connick Associates
Wilbur Herbert Burnham	Gregor T. Goethals,
Joseph G. Reynolds Associates, Belmont, Mass.	Monroe, Louisiana
	STATUES
ETCHED GLASS	Lee Lawrie,
Duncan Niles Terry	Easton, Maryland

oppressed of the city and of the world. And, just as Dr. Fosdick stood against war, Dr. Coffin led the congregation to study the ever-growing arms race and to consider its spiritual obligation to confront the "warring madness."

Dr. Coffin was always conscious of "the magnitude of inhuman behavior and its potential to destroy." Even so, his message was one of peacemaking in the biblical understanding of forgiveness, love, and justice.

In his sermons and his writings, he called for nations "to confer, not conquer, to discuss, not destroy, to extend olive branches, not their missile ranges."

On December 7, 1981, some 3500 persons—CBS-TV cameras and crew, busloads of students from New Jersey, religious leaders, a brass band, ambassadors to the United Nations, and children from the neighborhood—came together to hear a call to action on the theme, "The Threats to Global Security," dealing with such issues as militarism, poverty, and the calls for justice on the part of the oppressed. This was an evening sponsored by the Riverside Disarmament Program, which was launched during Coffin's years as Senior Minister.

On June 1, 1989, the Reverend Dr. James A. Forbes, Jr. was installed as the fifth Senior Minister of The Riverside Church, becoming the first African American to serve in that capacity. He is an ordained minister in the American Baptist Churches USA and in the Original United Holy Church of America. In honor of his installation at Riverside, Union Theological Seminary, where he had been on the faculty since 1976, named him their first Harry Emerson Fosdick Adjunct Professor of Preaching.

Photos left to right:
On June 21, 1990, Dr. Forbes welcomed Nelson Mandela, who came to Riverside for an interfaith service to thank the religious leaders of America for "the love and concern shown" during his long struggle for freedom.

One month after Dr. Forbes' sermon on emancipation from poverty, on February 18, 1997, President Bill Clinton came to Riverside to ask for the support of churches and businesses to support the government's welfare to work program.

During one of his annual trips to the United States, His Holiness the Dalai Lama spoke from the Riverside Chancel in a special lecture to his followers on Sunday, August 15, 1999. He is seen here exchanging gifts with Dr. Forbes.

With a strong prophetic vision, Dr. Forbes has carried on in the progressive tradition of his distinguished predecessors by fighting for the eradication of poverty, for racial and social justice, and for broad inclusivity. Indeed, the striking diversity of Riverside's congregation across lines of race, color, religion, gender, national origin, sexual orientation, age, and class now serves as a model and inspiration for congregations across the country and around the world.

> "The future of our world depends upon our learning to hear each other across the serious divides of religious intolerance."
>
> James A. Forbes, Jr.

By articulating a vision for Riverside of love and care for all of God's children, Dr. Forbes' message is one of personal growth leading to social transformation and culminating in the spiritual revitalization of the country. His theology is a forward-looking approach resonating with the redemptive themes of many traditions.

During the ministry of Dr. Forbes, leaders from across the nation and around the world have come to Riverside to engage in meaningful dialogue and to acknowledge the work of this thoughtful and visionary congregation. Important public discussions that have occurred at Riverside concerning health and wellness, multiculturalism, and the need to emancipate the poor from the debilitating effects of poverty have significantly affected public discourse on these issues. The Riverside Wellness Center, which grew out of one of those early dialogues and the work of the Comprehensive Health and Wellness Ministry, remains a center designed to serve and empower individuals toward God's call to wholeness.

Under the leadership of Dr. Forbes, in October 2000, the Church Congregation approved the formation of the Jubilee Fund, which will invest $10 million in support of programs in the areas of community development, healthcare, public education, and youth outreach. The Jubilee Fund represents Riverside's continuing commitment to its neighbors and to the Harlem community.

Peace, justice, the transforming power of the Spirit, Christian love, and social action—these are calls to The Riverside Church that transcend time and place. In these calls a member of this church becomes part of an ageless community of faith, constantly renewed, and ever growing in strength, and hope in God.

Clockwise from top left:

Dr. Forbes joined the Balm in Gilead with Jessye Norman (far right) and friends including (l. – r.) Bill T. Jones, Elton John, and Toni Morrison, on December 4, 1996, in a major benefit to fight HIV/AIDS. Also present but not shown were Whoopi Goldberg and Maya Angelou.

The Rev. Jesse Jackson, founder and president of The Rainbow/PUSH Coalition, a multi-issue organization working toward social, racial, and economic justice, has frequently preached at Riverside, including for Martin Luther King, Jr.'s Sunday service held in January each year.

Dr. Forbes and Executive Minister Dr. Bernard Wilson (l.) welcome Cuban President Fidel Castro to Riverside on September 8, 2000, for a gathering in support of Cuba.

Dr. Billy Jones, Church Council Chair (r.), presents a check for $10 million dollars to the Jubilee Fund Committee, which includes (l.-r.), Rev. James Stallings, Betty Davis, Rev. Bernard Wilson, and Jean Barber-Bucek.

In the aftermath of the tragic events of September 11, 2001, WNET/PBS and Riverside hosted an interfaith service for public broadcast. Included in the service were several religious leaders from the New York area including (l.-r.) Ven. T. Kenjitsu Nakagaki, a Sensai from the Buddhist Council of New York; Cantor Benji Ellen Schiller and Rabbi Lester Bronstein of Bet Am Shalom Synagogue; and Karda A-Quari Sheikh Ahmed Dewidar and Imam Al-Hajj W. Abur-Rashid of the Mosque of Islamic Brotherhood in New York.

The Exterior

The Riverside Church is situated at one of the highest points of New York City, overlooking the Hudson River at Riverside Drive and 122nd Street.

Surrounding the church are religious and educational institutions, public parks, and the neighboring communities of Harlem and Morningside Heights.

The Riverside Church's simple, bold design reflects the spirit of medieval religious art, but in a new expression adapted to the life and needs of this time.

Many European Gothic cathedrals played a part in the design of the church, but the major inspiration was Chartres Cathedral in France.

The building, spacious enough for today's expanded program, is beautiful as it recalls the tradition of an inspired religious age.

It is 100 feet wide and covers two city blocks. The tower, rising to a height of 392 feet, is the first of its kind to serve a functional purpose, providing 24 floors for the congregation's program.

The building is dedicated to a living ministry and to the glory of God.

Above the main door are seven kings associated with the ancient Hebrews and with Christian tradition: David, Solomon, Marcus Aurelius, Clovis, Constantine, Charlemagne, and Alfred.

Above the cloister door stand Paul as Faith, Francis as Hope, and Martin as Charity. Below them is Maaseiah, the Keeper of the Threshold.

Just above the ridge of the nave on the four corners of the tower, each in a niche with a canopy characteristic of Chartres Cathedral, are the four archangels: Gabriel (southwest), the messenger of God; Raphael (northwest, left), chief of the guardians; Uriel (southeast), an interpreter of prophecy; above the northeast corner, Michael, at his feet a javelin transfixing a dragon, Satan.

Statues of Paul, Albert Schweitzer (above), and Jane Addams, on the exterior of the south wing, exemplify the complete dedication of people to the service of God through service to others.

On a line with the roses of the clerestory apse windows are six niches holding the angels of the Apocalypse from the Book of Revelation: the cathedral, symbolic of the seven churches of the Apocalypse; the book sealed with the seven seals; the seal of the living God (left); the golden censer to loose the seven angels with seven pests; the trumpet and symbols of fire and water, representing the seven angels of destruction; the sealed book and rainbow, symbols of the sealing of the thunders and the prophecy that there will be no more time.

In the tradition of many European cathedrals, the architects of The Riverside Church planned a motif somewhat independent of its main conception.

The Woman's Porch, at the northwest corner, portrays four women of great faith: Mary and Martha face north, while Eunice and Lois look west.

"Madonna and Child" (1927) was regarded by Sir Jacob Epstein as one of the greatest works of his career. The bronze statue, given to The Riverside Church in 1960 by the American artist, Sally Fortune Ryan, emphasizes both the humanity of Jesus and the miracle of the incarnation.

From the garth, the two figures look over the street, challenging the church to look on this city with wisdom and compassion.

Above the chapel door, the horizontal top piece below the nativity scene shows the stages of life from birth to parenthood, symbolizing immortality. The arches, with symbols of the months of the year, suggest time, endlessly weaving the fabric of life.

In the tradition of ancient cathedrals, gargoyles defy human aims for perfection in the building of a cathedral church. The gargoyles of The Riverside Church stare below them, only emphasizing in their defiance the great heights the tower will reach.

In the wilderness prepare
the way of the Lord,
Make straight in the desert
a highway for our God!

Isaiah 40:3

"O Jerusalem, Jerusalem, killing the prophets and stoning those who are sent to you! How often would I have gathered your children together as a hen gathers her brood under her wings, and you would not!" (Matthew 23:37)

The figure of Christ represents the central thought in the story told in the west portal. Surrounding Christ are the symbols of the four evangelists: the Angel, Matthew; the Lion, Mark; the Eagle, John; and the Bull, Luke.

Below a band of clouds is a series of towers and turrets, suggestive of the cities of Jerusalem and New York.

A scene below represents the struggle between good and evil, continual in the lives of all people; below this are the twelve Apostles.

On each side of the door stand five figures who usher the congregation into the church: Old Testament prophets and New Testament friends of Jesus. Between the great wooden doors stands the disciple John.

20

The
Nave

"The beauty of proportion and perspective, of symbolism and color, would speak to the soul even when the voice...is silent."

Harry Emerson Fosdick

In The Riverside Church the strivings and aspirations of humanity pervade the nave, a tribute to its founders, architects, artists, and craftsmen, and to their dedication to the glory of God.

The sculpture and stained glass speak with confidence of the scientific advances of the early years of this century.

In the chancel screen, Luke of the Physicians Panel is flanked by such figures as Louis Pasteur, Andreas Vasalius, Joseph Lister, and Robert Koch. Christ as Teacher is surrounded by Socrates, Erasmus, and Pestalozzi. The tradition of the Good Samaritan reaches from Francis of Assisi to Abraham Lincoln, Florence Nightingale, and the Family Doctor.

The windows depict the historical development of agriculture, religious reform, government, scholarship, and internationalism.

Jesus is seen here as a person among a diverse company of men and women who have bettered humanity.

From the gallery, Christ in Majesty, everlasting strength and hope, rises above the congregation.

Come from the East and the West,
and from the North and the South, and
gather about the table of the Lord.

    Let us come to the table not because
we must, but because we may.

Jeremiah prophesies the destruction of Israel's enemies: the destruction of Babylon; figure symbolizing the repentance of Israel; the destruction of Damascus.

The story of Jeremiah, woven around the supporting pillars of the nave, is told in stone images that recall the picturesque style of the Old Testament prophet.

The story begins at the southwest corner of the nave and continues on the southeast pillar, alternating from one side of the nave to the other until it concludes at the two engaged pillars at the north end, one beside the pulpit and the other beside the lectern.

The first column (southwest) portrays the annointing of Jeremiah by Yahweh; the second, the contrast between the holy life in the wilderness and the life of Jeremiah's day in Jerusalem.

The succeeding pillars show prophecies of Jeremiah and the history of Israel before the fall of Jerusalem. The last free-standing pillars show the fall of Jerusalem and Jeremiah prophesying the destruction of Israel's enemies.

The pillars at the north wall depict the forgiveness of Israel and Judah, and the reward of righteousness.

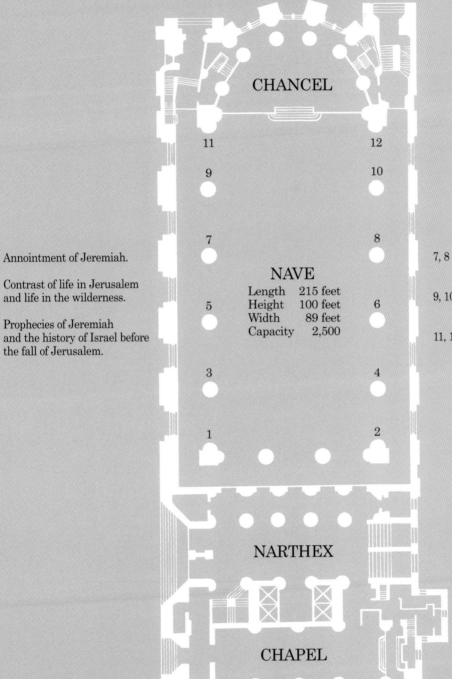

1   Annointment of Jeremiah.

2   Contrast of life in Jerusalem
      and life in the wilderness.

3, 4, 5, 6   Prophecies of Jeremiah
and the history of Israel before
the fall of Jerusalem.

CHANCEL

NAVE
Length   215 feet
Height   100 feet
Width   89 feet
Capacity   2,500

7, 8   The fulfillment of prophecies
and the fall of Jerusalem.

9, 10   Jeremiah's prophecies of the
destruction of Israel's enemies.

11, 12   Forgiveness and the reward
of righteousness.

NARTHEX

CHAPEL

The labyrinth on the floor of the chancel has been adapted from the labyrinth at Chartres, one of the few such medieval designs in existence.

Little is known of the significance of the labyrinth in the worship of the Middle Ages, except that many women and children followed the track on their knees.

The labyrinth may have been a reminder of the Via Dolorosa, Christ's route to Calvary. Or, it may have served as a substitute journey for the faithful who could not go on the Crusades.

Physicians

1. Andreas Vesalius
   (1514-1564)
2. Joseph Lister
   (1827-1912)
3. Robert Koch
   (1843-1910)
4. Hippocrates
   (c. 460 - c. 377B.C.)
5. Luke
6. Christ the Physician
7. Thomas Sydenham
   (1624-1689)
8. Louis Pasteur
   (1822-1895)

Teachers

1. Thomas Aquinas
   (c. 1225-1274)
2. Henry Drummond
   (1786-1860)
3. Thomas Arnold
   (1795-1842)
4. Socrates
   (c. 470 - 399 B.C.)
5. Christ the Teacher
6. Desiderius Erasmus
   (1465-1536)
7. Johann Heinrich
   Pestalozzi
   (1746-1827)

Prophets

1. Girolamo Savonarola
   (1452-1498)
2. John Ruskin
   (1819-1900)
3. Moses
4. Christ the Prophet
5. Isaiah
6. John the Baptist
7. Micah
8. Elijah
9. Elisha
10. Amos
11. Hosea

Humanitarians

1. Christ the Humanitarian
2. Francis of Assisi
   (1186-1226)
3. Elizabeth of Hungary
   (1207-1231)
4. Valentin Hauy
   (1745-1822)
5. Ann Judson
   (1789-1826)
6. Abraham Lincoln
   (1809-1865)
7. Booker T. Washington
   (1858-1915)
8. Samuel Chapman
   Armstrong (1839-1893)
9. The Good Samaritan

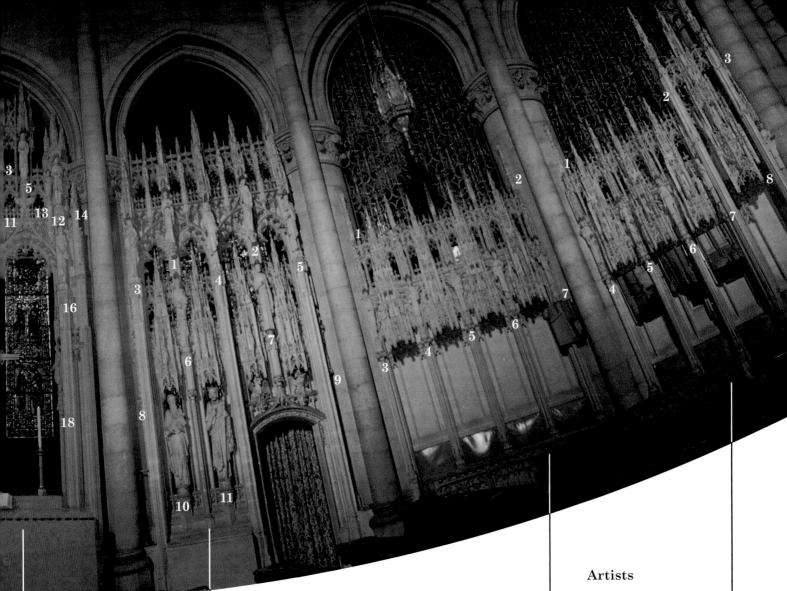

Missionaries

1. Philip the Evangelist
2. Stephen
   (c. 977-1038)
3. John Eliot
   (1604-1690)
4. Christ the Missionary
5. William Carey
   (1761-1834)
6. Augustine
   (354-430)
7. Francis Xavier
   (1506-1552)
8. Robert Morrison
   (1782-1834)
9. Adoniram Judson
   (1788-1850)
10. Paul
11. David Livingstone
    (1813-1873)

10. Earl of Shaftesbury
    (1801-1885)
11. Florence Nightingale
    (1820-1910)
12. The Family Doctor
13. Walter Reed
    (1851-1902)
14. Edward Jenner
    (1749-1823)
15. John Howard
    (1726-1790)
16. William Booth
    (1829-1912)
17. Mary the Mother
    of Jesus
18. John the Disciple

Reformers

1. George Fox
   (1624-1691)
2. John Knox
   (1505-1572)
3. John Wesley
   (1703-1791)
4. John Wycliffe
   (c. 1324-1384)
5. Christ the Reformer
6. Martin Luther
   (1483-1546)
7. John Calvin
   (1509-1564)

Artists

1. John Greenleaf
   Whittier
   (1807-1892)
2. Fra Angelico
   (1387-1455)
3. John Milton
   (1608-1674)
4. Giovanni Palestrina
   (c. 1524-1594)
5. Leonardo da Vinci
   (1452-1519)
6. Christ the
   Lover of Beauty
7. Michelangelo
   (1475-1564)
8. Johann Sebastian
   Bach (1685-1750)

The wood canopy over the pulpit displays the architectural motif of a medieval cathedral.

This detail is carried out in the carved stone of the pulpit and lectern, where canopies each show a feature characteristic of a cathedral of the Middle Ages.

The theme of the oak choir stalls is praise of God, inspired by the Psalms.

On the ends of the stalls are pictured the elements and living things upon which the psalmist calls in Psalm 148. The misericordi (wooden brackets on the underside of the stall seats) derive their names from the penitential opening words of Psalm 51. In early times such seats provided a convenient rest for the monks during their long hours of chanting the Psalms.

Three pieces of stone were used to carve the major parts of the pulpit, each weighing three tons when it arrived at the building. Five large figures of prophets in the canopies around the supporting column beneath the pulpit represent, from left to right, Anna, Amos, Isaiah, Hosea, and Miriam.

The cathedrals of the old world are represented in ten canopies of the pulpit rail: Toulouse, Albi, Chartres, Coutances, Notre Dame, Rheims, Tours, Bourges, Amiens, Rouen.

The pulpit is dedicated to the memory of Cornelius Woelfkin, pastor of the Park Avenue Baptist Church, "whose wise and progressive leadership made this church possible."

Four stone figures on the front of the first gallery represent people of the Old Testament: Moses, the patriarchs; Amos (left), the prophets; David, the kings; and Gideon, the judges.

The lectern, as the desk for the Bible, symbolically upholds and supports the Scriptures.

For this, parables were chosen; from left to right, the Lost Sheep, the Wise Virgin, and the Mustard Seed.

Here, as on the pulpit, canopy designs are from cathedrals of Europe: Strasbourg, Laon, and Lepine.

A bold eagle stands on the top rail of the lectern, here as the symbol of John the Evangelist.

The lectern was given in memory of Rufus P. Johnston, pastor of the Fifth Avenue Baptist Church.

The chancel rail portrays the interests, activities, and ceremonies expressed in the worship and service of the people.

Prayer	The Publican and the Pharisee
Prophecy	Isaiah, the lion and lambs
Evangelism	Paul on Mars Hill
Ministry	Moses and the Commandments
Ordination	Candidate and two elders
Dedication	Parents, child, and minister
Memorial	Woman at the tomb
Baptism	Charlemagne, bishop and knight
Communion	Christ with two Apostles, bread and wine
Immortality	Christ and Mary Magdalene in the garden
Creation	God and Adam
Hymnody	Angel trio
Marriage	Pastor and couple
Festival	Triumphal entry
Friendship	David and Jonathan
Patriotism	Joseph gives grain to his people
Sacrifice	Mary annointing the head of Christ
Forgiveness	Christ and the woman taken in adultery
New Testament	The Sermon on the Mount
Old Testament	The Ark of the Covenant

Let light shine out of darkness.

II Corinthians 4:6

The Windows

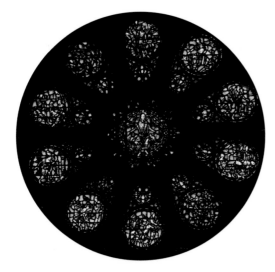

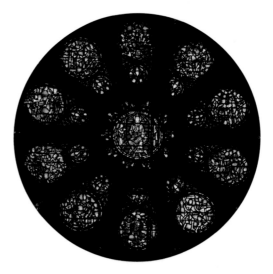

The east rose window represents ten parables. The center design is Christ in Glory. Reading to the left from the upper center are: the barren fig tree, sowing tares among the wheat, the talents, the Prodigal Son, the parable of the Good Samaritan, the vineyards, the rich man and Lazarus, the Good Shepherd, and the sower.

The west rose window shows the Ten Commandments, starting with the center design "I am the Lord thy God" as the first. The commandments continue just above the center design and clockwise around the rose.

The windows of The Riverside Church are a symphony of stained glass and color.

In the tradition of Chartres Cathedral, but made in the United States and France, they are the crowning glory to the magnificent architecture of the church.

Preserving an atmosphere of solemnity and mystery, the windows are contemporary in their interpretation of the Christian story.

Above the chancel, five apse clerestory windows are titled: Apostles, Jesse, Heavenly Host, Worship, and Praise. Below is the Mercy window.

The aisle clerestory windows symbolize the communion of God with humanity through Jesus Christ.

Many subjects of the aisle windows relate directly to modern history, but are treated in the Gothic spirit.

Holy Spirit Window (center), Apse Clerestory.

Francis is shown in the lower right medallion. Moses, beside him, holds the tablets of the law.
    In the middle section are Cecilia and Paul. John the Baptist is on the upper left with Chrysostom at his side.
    The emblem of the Holy Spirit is the central design of the rose above.

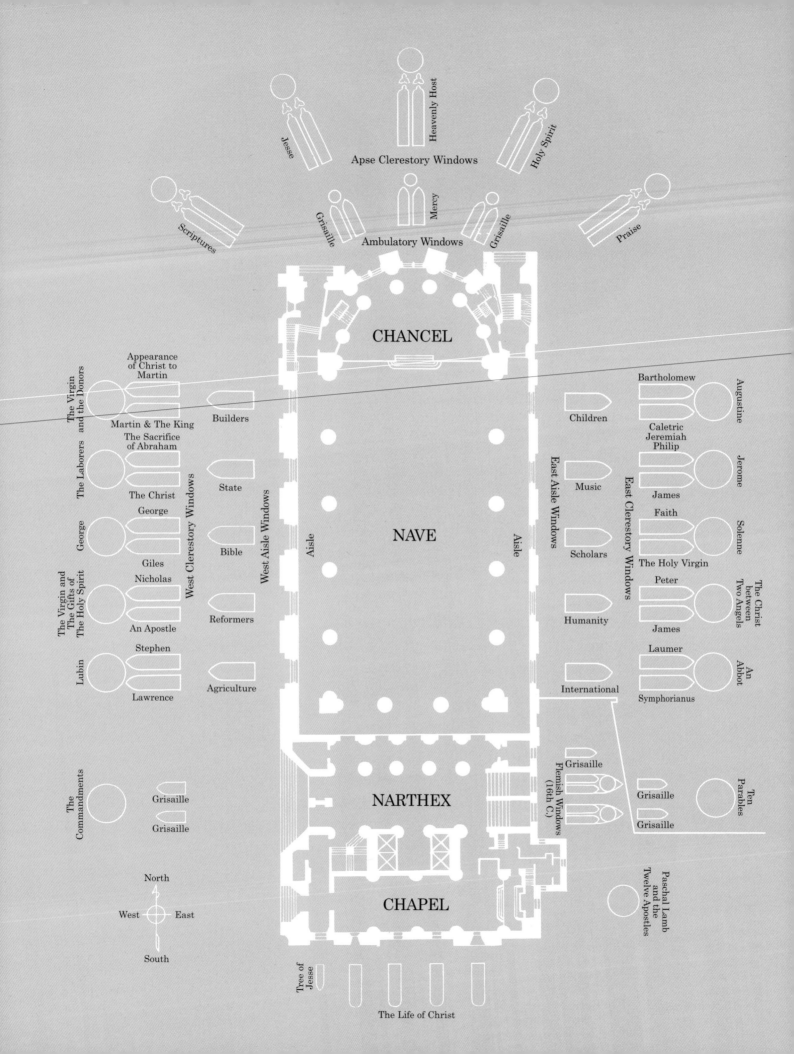

Jesse

Apse Clerestory Windows

Heavenly Host

Holy Spirit

Scriptures

Grisaille

Mercy

Grisaille

Praise

Ambulatory Windows

CHANCEL

Appearance
of Christ to
Martin

The Virgin
and the Donors

Martin & The King

Builders

Children

Bartholomew

Augustine

The Sacrifice
of Abraham

The Laborers

The Christ

State

Music

Caletric
Jeremiah
Philip

Jerome

George

George

West Clerestory Windows

Giles

West Aisle Windows

Bible

Aisle

NAVE

Aisle

East Aisle Windows

Scholars

James

Faith

East Clerestory Windows

Solenne

The Virgin and
The Gifts of
The Holy Spirit

Nicholas

The Holy Virgin

Peter

The Christ
between
Two Angels

An Apostle

Reformers

Humanity

James

Lubin

Stephen

Laumer

An
Abbot

Lawrence

Agriculture

International

Symphorianus

The
Commandments

Grisaille

NARTHEX

Grisaille

Flemish Windows
(16th C.)

Grisaille

Grisaille

Ten
Parables

Grisaille

North

West ✛ East

South

CHAPEL

Paschal Lamb
and the
Twelve Apostles

Tree of
Jesse

The Life of Christ

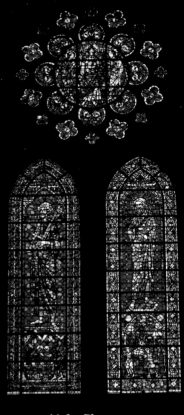

Aisle Clerestory
Rose: Virgin Mary and the Seven Gifts
of the Holy Spirit
Lancets: Apostle (l), Nicholas (r)

Aisle Clerestory
Rose: George
Lancets: Giles (l), George (r)

Aisle Clerestory
Rose: Christ between two angels
Lancets: Peter (l), James (r)

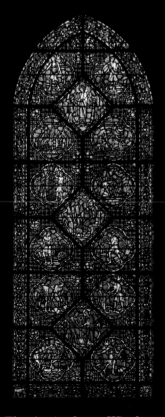

The Agriculture Window

The Bible Window

The Builders Window

The Music

Music in church is, like the building of great cathedrals and temples, an eternal song of praise to the glory of God.

The thoughts expressed in stone, stained glass, and wood are brought to life in music and in song.

Music educates and inspires the worshiper to respond.

Music enhances the role of the church as creator, sustainer, and protector of the arts.

The magnificent organs, six choirs, and carillon of The Riverside Church impel the church to present the finest music from a wide variety of musical periods, styles, and cultures.

The quality and variety of the musical resources and repertoire unite worshipers from many places and many walks of life, with each other and with God.

The sixty-five-voice Riverside Choir sings for all worship services and presents a number of major musical services every year.

The five-manual and pedal chancel console controls the total resources of the two nave organs (chancel and gallery).

The totally independent organ in the gallery has its own four-manual and pedal console.

Combined, the two organs have 203 ranks, more than 11,000 pipes and nearly 3,000 miscellaneous mechanical devices and controls.

God has gone up with a shout,
The Lord with the sound of a trumpet.

Psalm 47:5

The Trompeta Majestatis was dedicated Palm Sunday, 1978. It was given to The Riverside Church by Anthony A. Bufano in memory of his mother Virginia Rita de Marco Stark.

"Christ in Majesty," by Sir Jacob Epstein, is the gilded mold for the unique cast at Llandruff Cathedral in Cardiff, Wales. A gift to the church of Sally Fortune Ryan and Lady Epstein, it was dedicated on April 16, 1967. It measures 19-1/2 by 6 feet.

"That was more than a hymn to me when we sang it that day–it was a very urgent personal prayer. For with all my hopeful enthusiasm about the new venture there was inevitably much humble and sometimes fearful apprehension."

Harry Emerson Fosdick recalls the dedication of The Riverside Church, February 8, 1931. The hymn he wrote for that occasion is often sung on special days in the life of the congregation.

420 God of Grace and God of Glory

CWM RHONDDA 8.7.8.7.8.7.7

Harry Emerson Fosdick, 1930; alt.   John Hughes, 1907

1. God of grace and God of glo - ry, On Thy peo - ple
2. Lo! the hosts of e - vil round us Scorn Thy Christ, as -
3. Cure Thy chil - dren's war - ring mad - ness, Bend our pride to
4. Set our feet on loft - y pla - ces; Gird our lives that

pour Thy power; Crown Thine an - cient chur - ch's sto - ry;
sail Thy ways! From the fears that long have bound us
Thy con - trol; Shame our wan - ton, self - ish glad - ness,
they may be Ar - mored with all Christ - like gra - ces,

Bring its bud to glo-rious flower. Grant us wis - dom, grant us cour-age,
Free our hearts to faith and praise. Grant us wis - dom, grant us cour-age,
Rich in things and poor in soul. Grant us wis - dom, grant us cour-age,
Pledged to set all cap-tives free. Grant us wis - dom, grant us cour-age,

For the fac-ing of this hour, For the fac-ing of this hour.
For the liv-ing of these days, For the liv-ing of these days.
Lest we miss Thy king-dom's goal, Lest we miss Thy king-dom's goal.
That we fail not them nor Thee! That we fail not them nor Thee!

The Carillon

In the tower is one of the most notable carillons in the world.

The Laura Spelman Rockefeller Memorial Carillon was presented in 1925 to the Park Avenue Baptist Church by John D. Rockefeller, Jr., in memory of his mother.

For its move to The Riverside Church, it was enlarged from fifty-three bells to seventy-two. In 1955, fifty-six bells were sent to Holland to be recast and retuned. At that time two bells were added, bringing the total to seventy-four.

In 2000, 58 new bells were cast by Whitechapel Foundry to match the original bells.

The Bourdon Bell, weighing twenty tons, is the largest and heaviest tuned bell ever cast. The smallest bell weighs ten pounds.

In its size and weight, the Riverside carillon has never been surpassed.

The carillon is part of the rich ministry of music at The Riverside Church. Programs of sacred music are played before the morning service and recitals in the afternoon.

With the pealing of bells, the carillon tolls the sorrows and the joys of the community of The Riverside Church.

At the clavier, located in a cabin in the tower, are wooden hand levers and foot pedals.

The machine room controls automatic operations. Five of the larger bells are swung by wheels and electric motors.

All 74 bells can be played from the carillon keyboard.

Daily, the Bourdon Bell sounds the hours and automatically the carillon plays Wagner's "Parsifal Quarters."

Daily, the community surrounding The Riverside Church hears the call from the tower of bells.

The Bourdon Bell

46

Ring out wild bells to the wild sky
Ring out the thousand wars of old
Ring in the thousand years of peace
Ring out the darkness of the land
Ring in the Christ that is to be!

Alfred Lord Tennyson

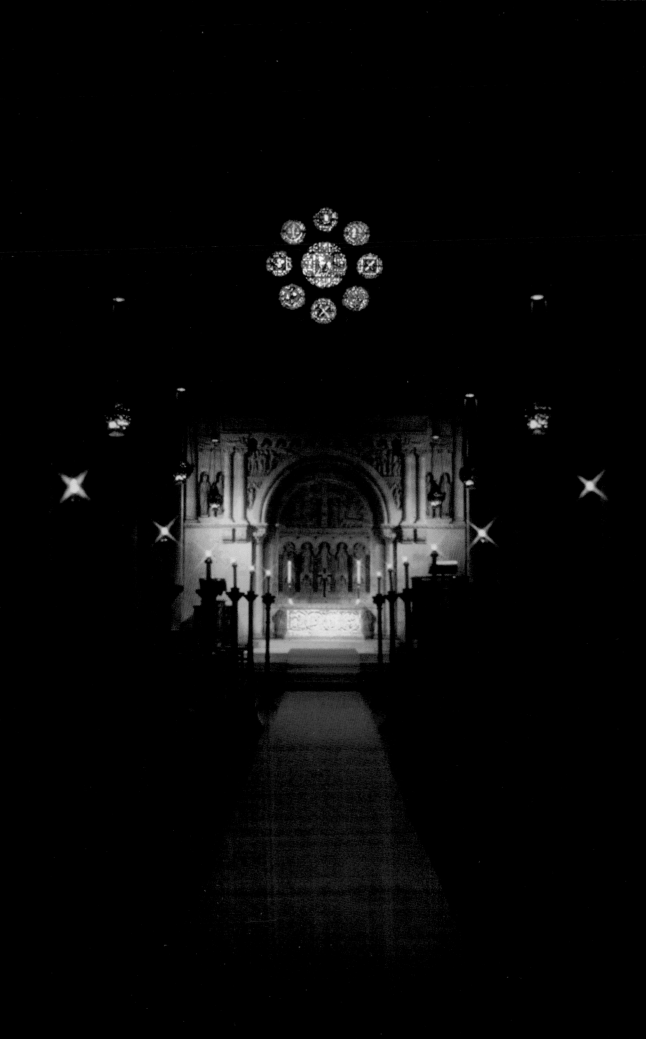

The Chapels

Worshipers gather in the chapels of The Riverside Church for weddings, funerals, church school services, and special celebrations.

The chapels are also places for quiet meditation and prayer.

Christ Chapel, patterned after the eleventh century Romanesque nave of the fortress church of St. Nazaire at Carcassonne, belongs architecturally to an earlier period than does the rest of the church.

The story of the life of Christ from the Annunciation to the Resurrection is told in stained glass in the Romanesque windows of the south wall.

Symbols of the apostles are the motif for the rose window and for the wrought iron doors.

The chapel's focal point, a stone-carved reredos forming the background of the altar, tells of the Last Supper and the Transfiguration and depicts Christ as Shepherd.

The inscription speaks boldly the biblical promise: "The truth shall set you free." (John 8:32)

Christ Chapel

The bold cross captures the interest of all who come to Christ Chapel. The portion above the arms of the cross represents the closed door of the sheepfold and itself constitutes a cross.

The symbol of the hand and the dove on either side represents the Father and the Holy Spirit, establishing the Trinity at the very top of the composition.

The interwoven border which frames the entire composition is peopled by the prophets who attend the Tree of Jesse in the famous window of that name in Chartres Cathedral: Christ, Isaiah, and Moses; Jeremiah, Ezekiel, and Samuel; Nahum, Daniel, and Baalim; Joel, Micah, Amos, and Hosea.

The Gethsemane Chapel was conceived as an alternate to a commercial mortuary chapel. An aperture admits light to the room, setting it aside as a place connected with life rather than death. The painting of "Christ in Gethsemane," by Heinrich Hofmann, was acquired for The Riverside Church by John D. Rockefeller, Jr., expressly for this chapel, a continuing comfort to the people who seek quiet and private meditation here.

On the third floor of the south wing is the Chapel of the Cross. Its dominant feature is a colorful mosaic mural behind the altar, whose dramatic design conveys the motion, vitality, and aspiration of the life of the city. In front of the mosaic is a wrought iron cross, symbolizing God's redeeming power at work in the city and world.

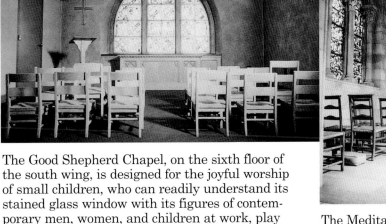

The Good Shepherd Chapel, on the sixth floor of the south wing, is designed for the joyful worship of small children, who can readily understand its stained glass window with its figures of contemporary men, women, and children at work, play and worship. Woven into the pattern are such familiar figures as a dog, a fish, a butterfly, an elephant, and a lamb. The man and woman at the top of the window signify a present day Joseph and Mary.

The Meditation Chapel, located off the cloister lounge, is a quiet place frequented by staff, members, and visitors to the church.

The Narthex

I n the narthex are the only original Renaissance windows in the church. The two 16th century Flemish windows are from a church probably threatened or destroyed during the French Revolution. Later the English inscriptions were added.

The two windows illustrate events, miracles, and parables in the life of Christ.

Two statues represent the church: the angel holding a cathedral (at right) as the temporal church; the angel with a chalice as the spiritual church.

Detail, Narthex Flemish Window

The Paintings

"Christ's Image"
was a gift of
Elise A. Drexel.

In The Riverside Church are paintings by
Heinrich Hofmann, three of them gifts of John
D. Rockefeller, Jr., which are widely known and
appreciated.

"Christ in Gethsemane" (1890) was pur-
chased by Mr. Rockefeller for the chapel then
named for it. There it has been a consolation
and inspiration to many visitors.

"Christ and the Rich Young Man" (1889)

"Christ in the Temple" (1871), a copy of the
original, was executed under the supervision
of Heinrich Hofmann.

"Christ in Gethsemane"

"Many members—a single body, differing gifts—one Spirit. This is the church as it was meant to be!"
Ernest T. Campbell

Seven Days a Week

The Riverside Church is a symbol and instrument of the conviction that Christian ministry must be the immediate result of Christian worship.

It is a living commitment to the daily demands of the people of the community who must be served —seven days a week.

The South Wing, dedicated in 1959, marked the culmination of plans for expansion that had been foreseen even prior to the building of the nave.

The church was expanded at a time when its members had clearly shown that they could use greater facilities in service to their congregation and the wider community.

The offer of John D. Rockefeller, Jr., to build and maintain an addition to the nave was unanimously and gratefully accepted by the congregation in 1955.

Mr. Rockefeller's dedication was met by the commitment of the Riverside congregation to support the expanding program that the new facilities would allow.

The wing opened new doors of possibility for the people of the neighborhood—church school, theater, social services, and a diverse program of education.

The South Wing was rededicated as the Martin Luther King, Jr. Memorial Wing on January 12,1985.

The Riverside Church enjoys unlimited opportunity: as a parish church; a cathedral church; a center for ministry to people and institutions of the community; and a meeting place for national and international organizations.

The membership is the authority for the policy, program, and administration of the church.

The work of the church is carried out by its members, clergy, and staff.

It is interdenominational, interracial, and international in membership.

The Riverside Church is affiliated with the American Baptist Churches USA and the United Church of Christ. It is legally independent and is incorporated under New York law as a Baptist Church.

The Riverside Church seeks a unity in Christ that celebrates the diversity of its people.

The affirmation of faith in Christ is the only requirement for membership.

MISSION STATEMENT
OF THE RIVERSIDE CHURCH IN THE CITY OF NEW YORK

The Riverside Church seeks to be a community of faith. Its members are united in the worship of God known in Jesus, the Christ, through the inspiration of the Holy Spirit. The mission of The Riverside Church is to serve God through word and witness; to treat all human beings as sisters and brothers; and to foster responsible stewardship of all God's creation.

The Riverside Church commits itself to welcoming all persons, celebrating the diversity found in a congregation broadly inclusive of persons from different backgrounds of race, economic class, religion, culture, ethnicity, gender, age, and sexual orientation. Members are called to an individual and collective quality of life that leads to personal, spiritual, and social transformation, witnessing to God's saving purposes for all creation.

Therefore, The Riverside Church pledges itself to education, reflection, and action for peace and justice, the realization of the vision of the heavenly banquet where all are loved and blessed.

Approved by the Religious Society of The Riverside Church on May 17, 1992.

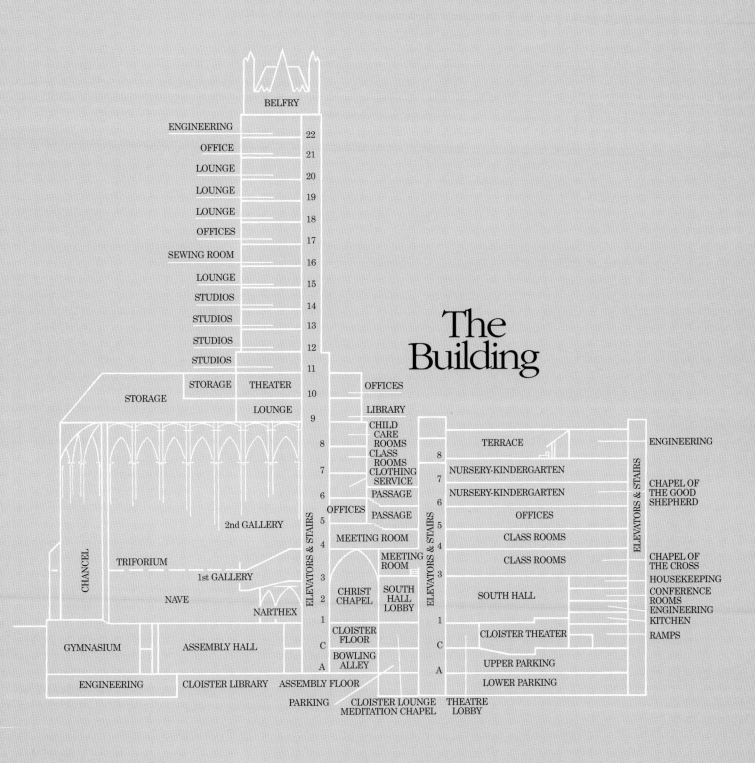

1 Theater
2 Kitchen, one of twenty
3 Hall of Churches
4 Roof playground
5 Cloister lounge

6 Nursery-Kindergarten room
7 Roof terrace
8 The Columbarium
9 Main Library, Cloister
10 Lounge, ninth floor tower
11 Ceramic tile, Roof terrace

63

1 South Hall Lobby
2 Window, Hall of
   Churches
3 Library, ninth floor
4 Gymnasium
5 Cloister

6 Stone Gym
7 Studio
8 Assembly Hall
9 Nursery-Kindergarten room
10 Ceramic tile, Roof Terrace

Afterword

If all over the world, at home and abroad, wherever the Kingdom of God is hard bestead, the support of this church should be felt and, like an incoming tide, many an estuary of human need should feel its contribution flowing in, that would be wonderful.

If young men and women, coming to that church should have Isaiah's experience, seeing the Lord high and lifted up, his train filling the temple, and if they too should discover their divine vocation...that would be wonderful.

If, wherever soldiers of the common good are fighting for a more decent international life and a just industry, they should feel behind them the support of this church, which, though associated in the public thought with prosperity and power, has kept its conviction clear that a major part of Christianity is the application of the principles of Jesus to the social life, and that no industrial or international question is ever settled until it is settled Christianly, that would be wonderful.

And if in this city, this glorious, wretched city, where so many live in houses that human beings ought not to live in, where children play upon streets that ought not to be the children's playground, where unemployment haunts families like the fear of hell and two weeks in the country in the summertime is a paradise for a little child, if we could lift some burdens and lighten some dark spots and help to solve the problems of some communities, that would be wonderful.

If in that new temple we simply sit together in heavenly places, that will not be wonderful, but if we also work together in unheavenly places, that will be.

Harry Emerson Fosdick

This book was set in
Garamond Light and Century Schoolbook by Summit Marketing.
It was printed by Maar Printing Service.
Diagrams were drawn by John Allen.
The windows were photographed by Hal H. Conroy.

The Riverside Church
490 Riverside Drive
New York, N.Y. 10027
www.theriversidechurchny.org